Will Shortz Presents

BRAIN-BUSTING
KENKEN®

"KenKen®: Logic Puzzles That Make You Smarter":

Will Shortz Presents KenKen Easiest, Volume 1
Will Shortz Presents KenKen Easy, Volume 2
Will Shortz Presents KenKen Easy to Hard, Volume 3
Will Shortz Presents The Little Gift Book of KenKen
Will Shortz Presents Crazy for KenKen Easiest
Will Shortz Presents Crazy for KenKen Easy
Will Shortz Presents Crazy for KenKen Easy to Hard
Will Shortz Presents KenKen for the Seaside
Will Shortz Presents KenKen for Your Coffee Break
Will Shortz Presents KenKen for Stress Relief
Will Shortz Presents Tame KenKen
Will Shortz Presents Wild KenKen
Will Shortz Presents Ferocious KenKen
Will Shortz Presents The Ultimate KenKen Omnibus
Will Shortz Presents KenKen for Your Vacation
The New York Times Will Shortz Presents
Easy to Hard KenKen
The New York Times Will Shortz Presents
Challenging KenKen
The New York Times Will Shortz Presents
Diabolical KenKen
Will Shortz Presents The Little Pink Book of KenKen
Will Shortz Presents The Big, Bad Book of KenKen
Will Shortz Presents The Monster Book of KenKen
Will Shortz Presents KenKen Lovers Only: Easy Puzzles
Will Shortz Presents KenKen Lovers Only:
Easy to Hard Puzzles

KenKen for Kids

Will Shortz Presents I Can KenKen! Volume 1
Will Shortz Presents I Can KenKen! Volume 2
Will Shortz Presents I Can KenKen! Volume 3

WILL SHORTZ PRESENTS
BRAIN-BUSTING

KENKEN®

100 CHALLENGING LOGIC PUZZLES THAT MAKE YOU SMARTER

TETSUYA MIYAMOTO

INTRODUCTION BY
WILL SHORTZ

ST. MARTIN'S GRIFFIN
NEW YORK

WILL SHORTZ PRESENTS BRAIN-BUSTING KENKEN®. KenKen® is a registered trademark of Nextoy, LLC © 2011, KenKen Puzzle LLC. Introduction © 2011 by Will Shortz. All rights reserved. Printed in the United States of America. For information, address St. Martin's Press, 175 Fifth Avenue, New York, N.Y. 10010.

www.stmartins.com

ISBN 978-0-312-68143-2

First Edition: February 2011

10 9 8 7 6 5 4 3 2 1

Introduction

If you consider all the world's greatest puzzle varieties, the ones that have inspired crazes over the years—crosswords, jigsaw puzzles, tangrams, sudoku, etc.—they have several properties in common. They . . .

- Are simple to learn
- Have great depth
- Are variable in difficulty, from easy to hard
- Are mentally soothing and pleasing
- Have some unique feature that makes them different from everything else and instantly addictive

By these standards, a new puzzle called KenKen, the subject of the book you're holding, has the potential to become one of the world's greats.

KenKen is Japanese for "square wisdom" or "cleverness squared." The rules are simple: Fill the grid with digits so as not to repeat a digit in any row or column (as in sudoku) and so the digits within each heavily outlined group of boxes combine to make the arithmetic result indicated.

The simplest KenKen puzzles start with 3×3 boxes and use only addition. Harder examples have larger grids and more arithmetic operations.

KenKen was invented in 2003 by Tetsuya Miyamoto, a Japanese math instructor, as a means to help his students learn arithmetic and develop logical thinking. Tetsuya's education method is unusual. Put simply, he doesn't teach. His philosophy is to make the tools of learning available to students and then let them progress on their own.

Tetsuya's most popular learning tool has been KenKen, which his students spend hours doing and find more engaging than TV and video games.

It's true that KenKen has great capacity for educating and building the mind. But first and foremost it's a puzzle to be enjoyed. It is to numbers what the crossword puzzle is to words.

So turn the page and begin. . . .

—Will Shortz

How to Solve KenKen

KenKen is a logic puzzle with simple rules:

- Fill the grid with digits so as not to repeat a digit in any row or column.
- Digits within each heavily outlined group of squares, called a cage, must combine to make the arithmetic result indicated.
- A 3×3–square puzzle will use the digits from 1 to 3, a 4×4–square puzzle will use the digits from 1 to 4, etc.

Solving a KenKen puzzle involves pure logic and mathematics. No guesswork is needed. Every puzzle has a unique solution.

In this volume of KenKen, the puzzles use all four arithmetic operations—addition, subtraction, multiplication, and division—in the following manner:

- In a cage marked with a plus sign, the given number will be the sum of the digits you enter in the squares.
- In a cage marked with a minus sign, the given number will be the difference between the digits you enter in the squares (the lower digit subtracted from the higher one).
- In a cage marked with a multiplication sign, the given number will be the product of the digits you enter in the squares.
- In a cage marked with a division sign, the given number will be the quotient of the digits you enter in the squares.

Take this 5 × 5–square example.

48×		3+		4−
	8+	10×	4+	
3−				2÷
	4+		4	
7+			15×	

To start, fill in any digits in 1 × 1 sections—in this puzzle, the 4 in the fourth row. These are literally no-brainers.

Next, look for sections whose given numbers are either high or low, or that involve distinctive combinations of digits, since these are often the easiest to solve. For example, the L-shaped group in the upper left has a product of 48. The only combination of three digits from 1 to 5 that multiplies to 48 is 3, 4, and 4. Since the two 4s can't appear in the same row or column, they must appear at the ends of the L. The 3 goes between them.

Now look at the pair of squares in the first row with a sum of 3. The only two digits that add up to 3 are 1 and 2. We don't know their order yet, but this information can still be useful.

Sometimes, the next step in solving a KenKen puzzle is to ignore the given numbers and use sudoku-like logic to avoid repeating a digit in a row or column. For example, now that 1, 2, 3, and 4 have been used or are slated for use in the first row, the remaining square (at the end of the row) must be a 5. Then the digit below the 5 must be a 1 for this pair of squares to have a difference of 4.

Next, consider the pair of squares in the third column with a product of 10. The only two digits from 1 to 5 that have a product of 10 are 2 and 5. We don't know their order yet. However, the digit in the square above them, which we previously identified as either a 1 or a 2, must be 1, so as not to repeat a 2 in this column. The 2 that accompanies the 1 goes to its right.

Continuing in this way, using these and other techniques left for you to discover, you can work your way around the grid, filling in the rest of the squares. The complete solution is shown on the following page.

48× 3	4	**3+** 1	2	**4−** 5
4	**8+** 5	**10×** 2	**4+** 3	1
3− 2	3	5	1	**2÷** 4
5	**4+** 1	3	**4** 4	2
7+ 1	2	4	**15×** 5	3

Additional Tips

- In advanced KenKen puzzles, as you've seen, cages can have more than two squares. It's okay for a cage to repeat a digit—as long as the digit is not repeated in a row or column.
- Cages with more than two squares will always involve addition or multiplication. Subtraction and division occur only in cages with exactly two squares.
- Remember, in doing KenKen, you never have to guess. Every puzzle can be solved by using step-by-step logic. Keep going, and soon you'll be a KenKen master!

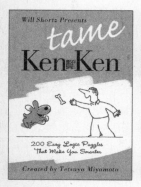

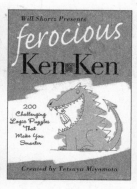
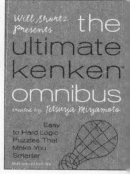

Moderate +/−/×/÷ 1

1 1	**1−** 4	**30×** 5	2	3
2− 5	3	**3+** 2	1	**2−** 4
3	**6+** 5	**3−** 1	**1−** 4	2
2÷ 2	1	4	3	**25×** 5
4	**1−** 2	3	5	1

345

9+	2−	2÷	10×	
4	3	1	2	5
5	1	2	12× 3	4
6+ 1	15+ 2	4	5	2− 3
2	9+ 5	2− 3	4	1
3	4	5	1− 1	2

345

Moderate +/−/×/÷ **3**

3 3	9+ 5	4	4× 1	2
2÷ 1	2− 3	30× 5	2	1− 4
2	1	3	7+ 4	5
1− 5	4	2	3	2− 1
8× 4	2	1	5 5	3

4 Moderate +/−/×/÷

24×		6+	2−	
2	4	5	3	1
3	9+ 2	1	20× 4	5
3− 4	5	2	4− 1	1− 3
1	15× 3	7+ 4	5	2
5	1	3	2÷ 2	4

1 3 5   2 3 4

2 3

Moderate +/−/×/÷ 5

2÷ 4	11+ 3	10× 1	5	2
2	4	3	1	60× 5
5× 5	1	2÷ 4	2	3
1	7+ 2	5	1− 3	4
2− 3	5	2 2	4	1

1 3 4 5

6 Moderate +/−/×/÷

1−		60×			2÷
			5		
2÷	2−		2−		
	20×		11+	12×	1−
		4	5		
540×	3+				
	6	2	1		
	6	11+		6×	
5					
				5+	
3					

5)540
6)1 0⁺8
   6)18
      3

6× 6	1	7+ 4	3	3− 5	2
1	40× 2	5	4	2÷ 6	3
24× 2	5 5	1	11+ 6	1− 3	4
4	36× 3	6 6	5	2÷ 2	4− 1
3	6	2	2÷ 1	4	5
12+ 5	4	3	2	6× 1	6

5 — 4 — 3
6 — 5 — 1

12/12/13

8 Moderate +/−/×/÷

6× 2	1	1− 6	5	1− 3	4
3	2÷ 2	1	5− 6	14+ 4	5
1 4	3	3− 2	1	5	2÷ 6
5− 1	6	5	9+ 4	2	3
15+ 6	60× 5	4	3	4+ 1	2
5	4	3	3÷ 2	6	1

5 | 60/12

12/12/13   345

Moderate +/−/×/÷ 9

20× 5₄	4₅	7+ 2	2− 3	1	24× 6₄
2÷ 2	1₂	5	3− 6	3	4₆
1− 3₃	3+ 2₄	1₂	2− 4	1− 6	5
4₄	1− 6	7+ 3	2	4− 5	1
5− 6₆	5	4	2÷ 1	2	5+ 3₂
1₁	2÷ 3	6	1− 5	4	2₃

123

12/12/13

2 45

10 Moderate +/−/×/÷

3−	2÷		2−		36×
	4−		30×	3÷	6
1−	10+ 4				2
2	6	3÷ 1	3	1 4	5
1−	10+	3÷ 6	2	1 1	5+ 4
			7+		1

3456

11+	10+	20×	5−		2÷
5	3	4	6	1	2
6	1	5	1− 3	2	4
120× 2	6	4	1− 5	4	3÷ 3
3	5	10+ 2	8× 4	90× 6	1
4	2	6	1	3	5
12× 1	4	3	2	30× 5	6

3

1

1   3   4   5   6

5/90/18   march 6 2014

12 Moderate +/–/×/÷

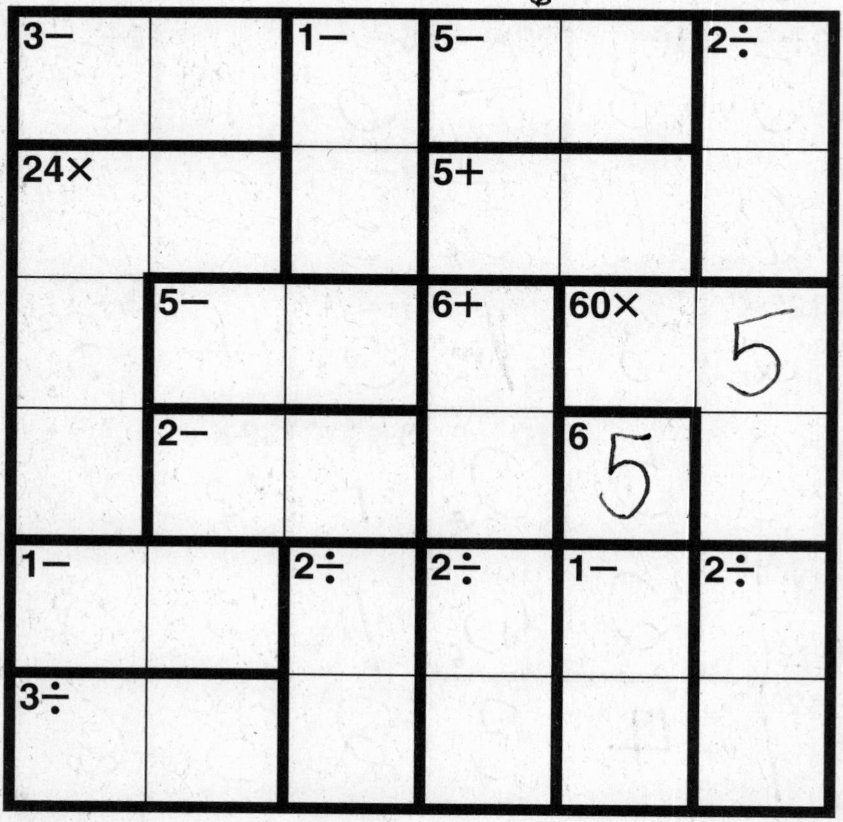
3–
1–
5–
2÷
24×
5+
5–
6+
60×
2–
6
1–
2÷
2÷
1–
2÷
3÷

Moderate +/−/×/÷ 13

2− 2	**3÷** 3	**10×** 5	**5+** 4	1	**1−** 6
4	1	2	**2−** 3	**2−** 6	5
2÷ 3	**5−** 6	1	5	4	**1−** 2
6	**2÷** 4	**3−** 3	**9+** 2	**12+** 5	1
100× 5	2	6	1	3	4
1	5	4	6	**6×** 2	3

4/1/14

14 Moderate +/−/×/÷

2÷ 2	1	**60×** 5	3	**3−** 4	**11+** 6
120× 3	2	**6** 6	4	1	5
4	**2−** 6	**1−** 2	**5** 5	**3÷** 3	1
5	4	1	**3÷** 2	6	**1−** 3
5− 6	**2−** 5	3	**10+** 1	2	4
1	**72×** 3	4	6	5	2

1/4/14

due

124

2 3 4 5

5)120
    24

4 7 2
    18

Moderate +/−/×/÷ 15

4−		2−		1−	2÷
3−	1−		5−		
	3	9+		3−	
11+			12×	5+	
11+				6	4−
2		12+			

16 Demanding +/−/×/÷

1−		1−		24×	5−
12+		30×			
	4			1−	
2÷	1−		20×		1−
	3−		3÷		
8+				3−	

Demanding +/−/×/÷ 17

7+	3−		5−	1−	48×
	3÷	7+			
11+			2÷		
		3÷	2−		1
30×			1−		8+
6		8×			

18 Demanding +/−/×/÷

1−		1−		2÷	
2÷		5−		3	15×
5−	2−		7+	4−	
	3−				48×
2−		2÷	17+		
6+					

Demanding +/−/×/÷ 19

6+	72×		1−		2÷
		12+		7+	
2−			2		15+
2−		60×		4	
4−	2÷			11+	
		3−			

20 Demanding +/−/×/÷

540×	10+			1−	
			2÷		3−
24×	3−		5−		
		60×	13+		
			10×		3
12×				1−	

Demanding +/−/×/÷ 21

1−		6+			80×
12+	60×		7+		
	2÷			54×	
		12+			2
24×		12+			
				30×	

22 Demanding +/−/×/÷

40×		2÷		7+	15×
2÷		4−			
	5−		13+	3−	2−
6+					
	2÷		10+	2÷	5−
6×					

Demanding +/−/×/÷ 23

18×	10+		48×		
	6×		2−		2−
		5+	6+	30×	
1−					9+
17+		6		2÷	
		3−			

24 Demanding +/−/×/÷

3÷		40×			15×
7+			5−		
2−	60×		3−		
		3÷		3÷	
6+			18+		2÷
30×					

Demanding +/−/×/÷   25

3÷	3−	5+		3−	
		60×			3÷
1−	1−	4−	3÷		
			7+		48×
4−	6+				
	60×			1−	

26 Demanding +/−/×/÷

30×	2÷		2÷		3−
	8+	9+	5−		
				9+	3÷
2−		5−			
2÷		9+		2÷	
2÷		6+		2−	

2÷		1−		3÷	
14+	40×			6×	
	6+			11+	3−
	1−				
2÷	2÷	20×	4−		4
				2−	

28 Demanding +/−/×/÷

75×		5−		2÷	
3−		2	15+		1−
	3−	3÷		30×	
24×					6
		11+		6+	2−
13+					

Demanding +/−/×/÷ 29

5−	3−	200×		2÷	
				7+	
1−	2÷		6+		
	30×	9+	10+		1−
				1	
3−		2÷		5+	

30 Demanding +/−/×/÷

4−		6+	2−		60×
1−	108×		10+		
				7+	
		10+		30×	1
2÷			1		
1−		11+		5+	

Very Challenging +/−/×/÷ 31

2÷		1−	11+		8×
5+				3÷	
	2−		1−		
2÷		8×		1−	
13+			11+	2−	
				2−	

32 Very Challenging +/−/×/÷

12+		15×		12×	
	150×			11+	
2−		8+	2−		
					2−
2÷	11+		24×	15×	
					5

Very Challenging +/−/×/÷ 33

2−	2÷	13+	1−		5−
			20×		
3÷				8+	10×
13+		3−			
	7+	3−	17+		1−

34 Very Challenging +/−/×/÷

2−		4−		1−	
6	7+	1−		12+	
		60×		1−	
	12+		4		2÷
7+		1−	7+	2÷	
					1

Very Challenging +/−/×/÷ 35

60×	1	10+	1−		2−
	15×		2÷		
		24×		3÷	2−
8+					
288×		10+	6+		2
			3−		

Very Challenging +/−/×/÷

60×			3÷		9+
2÷		60×	8+		
5−				20×	
3÷				1−	24×
60×		2−			
	11+			1−	

15×	7+	36×	4−		4
				12+	2÷
72×		2−			
	2÷		2÷		13+
1−		20×	2−		
				2÷	

12×		2	12+		
20×		24×		11+	
			1−		3÷
24×	1−			4−	
	2÷	8+			4×
		1−			

Very Challenging +/−/×/÷ 39

11+	2−	3−		24×	
		2÷			48×
8+			1−		
	2÷		1−	9+	
	30×				
1−		3÷		4−	

40 Very Challenging +/−/×/÷

4−	36×		2−		2−
	15+		5−		
2÷		11+	3−	3−	
				9+	3÷
7+					
	13+			3÷	

Very Challenging +/−/×/÷ 41

40×		14+	5+	7+	1−
3	5+	2÷		12+	24×
		17+			
18+				2−	
				3−	

42 Very Challenging +/−/×/÷

6+		10×	36×		1−
2−	2÷				
		8+		150×	
9+				1−	
2÷		30×			4×
12+					

6+		3	2÷	24×	
2−	2÷			2−	
	3−		2÷		3−
11+		11+	3÷		
2÷				1	3−
	2−		2−		

44 Very Challenging +/−/×/÷

11+		12×		4−	
2−		12+		30×	
	2÷	5+		2	
2−			11+	24×	
	20×			3−	
		3−		3−	

Very Challenging +/−/×/÷ 45

40×	5−		11+	1−	
	1−			12×	
	11+			6+	
18×	60×	2÷			72×
			2−		
	3÷			1−	

46 Moderate +/−/×/÷

90×			2−	6−	2−	
	5−	108×			3−	
2÷				3+		90×
	3−		3−	5		
42×	12+			11+		
		10+	9+		5−	
				105×		

Moderate +/−/×/÷ 47

35×	84×		10+			10+
	13+			48×		
		1−			1−	
10+		6−			1−	12+
			10+			
2−		8+		6−		2÷
60×			1−		2	

48 Moderate +/−/×/÷

30×		13+	6−		2÷	
				72×		2−
24×	42×		1−			
			5	2÷	21×	
1−		14×	13+		60×	
6−	2−					12+
		1−				

Moderate +/−/×/÷   49

10×			16+	11+		3÷
2−	12+				90×	
		3+		1−		
3÷		13+			6	56×
2÷			7+		6−	
	4	22+	4−	3÷		
					3−	

50 Moderate +/−/×/÷

2−	3−	3−	24×		3÷	
			3+		3÷	1−
1−		1	16+			
3÷	1−			13+	4−	
	30×	11+			9+	
8+				1−		2−
	10+		15×		7	

Moderate +/−/×/÷ 51

126×	3−		15×		3÷	
		12+		84×	6+	
6−		8+				2÷
10×			28×	1−		
2÷	11+	13+			3−	1−
			3−			
6			3−		2−	

52 Moderate +/−/×/÷

1−	17+		2÷		15×	
		1−	5−	11+	2÷	
3÷	10×				30×	
		72×		1−		
1−		5		2−	3−	
1−		28×	9+			2÷
2÷					2÷	

210×		1−		1−	3−	35×
	3÷		13+			
2−	8+	5		3+		
			3−	15+	2÷	
2−	420×				3−	
	6×		10+		15×	3÷
7						

54 Moderate +/−/×/÷

60×	2−	13+		3÷		1−
		7+	3÷	2÷	1−	
						16×
13+	2−	14+				
		8+		5+		1−
3÷		2−	3−		13+	
3÷			2−			

2−		28×		3÷		11+
5−		3÷		90×		
3−		9+	35×			
13+			1−		2−	
		8+		3−	3−	
10×		2−			10+	
2−		10+			6−	

56 Moderate +/−/×/÷

40×		2÷		3−		2−	20+
2÷		2÷		7−			
6×		28×		40×	6		
2÷			3−		42×		54×
5−	2−	2−		13+			
		336×			3+	4÷	
3−						6+	
7−		3−		280×			

Moderate +/−/×/÷ 57

4−	2−		80×		9+		
	20+			140×		84×	
		240×	3+			16+	
			15+		3−		3÷
21+			1−				
30×		3	504×		3−		4÷
	4−			7−		768×	
		5−		3			

58 Moderate +/−/×/÷

3+		2−	48×	42×		3−	1680×
2−	11+				1−		
		2÷	8+				
15+			1−	21×			2÷
	4÷			24×		3−	
4÷	2−		6×		6−		3−
	1680×	60×				2	
			13+			3÷	

4÷	1−	30×		3÷	26+		
		3+			2−		15+
24+		7	2÷			12+	
7			48×				
3÷	30×			42×			8
		3−		3−		4−	1−
9+		13+	336×				
2−				5−		1−	

60 Moderate +/−/×/÷

60×	14×		40×			2÷	
			13+	1−		1−	15+
3÷	3−			3+			
		9+		2÷		7−	
120×		2−	2−		2÷		2÷
15+			17+	3÷		6	
	16×				3−		2−
5−			5−		3−		

21×	3÷		400×	4+		1−	
	14+				7−		42×
7−		1−		1	1−	140×	
	15+		14+				
12+		8+		1−	3−		2−
		15+				2−	
13+	13+			9+			2÷
			3−		2÷		

62 Moderate +/−/×/÷

2	15+		1−	3÷	1−		64×
3−	2−			24×			
	2÷	3−			210×		
12×	4÷	4−	3−				
	140×		3÷		3−		
480×		11+		15+	7+		
	5−					6−	
	2−		8	5+			

Moderate +/−/×/÷ 63

96×		4	60×		1−	42×	
	3−	5+					3÷
10×		17+			3+		
	13+		7−		40×	14+	2÷
3÷	3+		1−				
	11+	7−	14+	13+			13+
3−					2÷	3−	
	2−						

64 Moderate +/−/×/÷

126×		3+		1−		12×	2−
		1680×			8+		
1−	15+					9+	
	64×		84×		2÷		
11+		15+		2−	15+		3+
			7−		16+		
2÷	3÷			13+		1−	
	3−		3			1−	

Moderate +/−/×/÷ 65

84×		2÷		7−		1680×	
	12+	6×	16+				
				140×		7+	96×
3÷	2−		3+				
	3÷		18+		48×	7	
392×				17+		72×	2÷
1−							
4÷		20×		4−			

66 Demanding +/−/×/÷

24×	2−		24+		6+	1−	5−
		1−					
4÷			140×			5−	10+
16+	5	4÷	54×				
				17+		2÷	
2÷	48×		3−				120×
		3−		4÷	7−	3−	
2−		3÷					

Demanding +/−/×/÷ 67

288×		16+	5−		1−		20×
				4÷	4−	2−	
21+	4−	1−					
		1−	2−		7−		36×
	8×		18+			4÷	
1		2÷	1−	1−	6−		
20×						22+	
	3−		9+		2÷		

68 Demanding +/−/×/÷

5−		5−		6+		10+	384×
2−		14+		4÷			
32×		18+		35×			
	3−			56×	7+		
6						18+	15×
24×		20+					
21×		13+		15+	1−		
						56×	

Demanding +/−/×/÷   69

35×	1−	15×	17+			7−	
			96×				2−
48×		196×		30×			
	26+		40×	2÷	19+		
					11+		
4÷		4÷		7+			120×
		12×			2−	9+	
10+			2−				

70 Demanding +/−/×/÷

30×		84×			7−		2÷
5−		6−		3−		2−	
4÷	14+	2−	336×				21×
			18+		2÷		
4−		19+			17+	2−	1
							48×
3−	7+	10+				20+	
		2÷		3−			

3÷	320×	10+				4−	3−
			36×	84×	13+		
2÷						5−	1−
	84×	5−					
		60×			12+	11+	3÷
105×		9+		8			
	15+		18+			192×	6−
1							

72 Demanding +/−/×/÷

35×	26+	1−		3÷	18+	2÷	
		6−					5−
3÷		30×		7+		10+	
		16+	7−	4−			
16+					8+	12+	
	2÷	21×		13+			2÷
		15+			784×		
	1−					2−	

Demanding +/−/×/÷ 73

1−		2÷	3−	12×		4÷	
2÷	12+			4	42×		13+
			14+	15+			
4−					30×		3−
2−	5−	2÷		7−			
		2−		2÷		7−	
17+			10+	2−	5−	2÷	3−
5−							

74 Demanding +/−/×/÷

280×	1−		144×		16+	1−	4÷
	7−	2÷					
			168×			48×	
3÷	18+		35×		32×		
	2−			40×			4−
10+		21×		7−	4÷		
			20+		120×		
1−					13+		

Demanding +/−/×/÷ 75

160×			11+			1−	2÷
2−		8+		8+			
3÷	2−	7−		15+			42×
		420×			2÷		
6−		11+				3−	
4÷	4−		16+		15×	1−	
		8					11+
30×		14×		5−			

76 Moderate +/−/×/÷

1−	2÷		1−	18+	2÷		294×	
	2−	4−				18×		
3−			6−	2−		16+	216×	
	4×	4		2−				
		7−			36×		3−	
648×	2−		2÷	3+		9+		5−
		360×			294×		1−	
			3	120×				3−
21+						8−		

Moderate +/−/×/÷ 77

11+	4−	30×		11+	8−		15+	
		1−	3+		14+	2−		
7	15+					120×		
		1−	240×		10+		8−	
240×				22+	11+		9+	1−
		4÷			144×	35×		
11+			5−					672×
1−	8−		5−	6×		8		
	30×					8+		

78 Moderate +/−/×/÷

6048×			2÷		3+	20+	7−	30×
		21+						
48×			140×				2	
168×		3+		18+			5−	
8−		96×		6−	3−	480×		
	12+					84×		
30×		126×		4÷	15+	30×		8−
	72×	2÷						
			10+			168×		

24×	294×			9	24×		1−	
		3−		2÷		7+		63×
30×		3÷			48×	21+		
2÷	864×	14+	42×					
			17+	3÷	2−		5−	
		3			1−		42×	4÷
17+		2÷	4÷	3−				
8−				1−		63×	1−	
		1−		1−			3−	

4−		3÷	48×		56×		18×	
11+			28×		4−		17+	7−
24×		10×		19+		17+		
	15+		12+				2÷	1−
21+				4−	8−	5		
	14+					2−	13+	
252×		120×		72×			35×	
	1−			2	120×			2÷
		1−		6×				

Moderate +/−/×/÷ 81

28×		4÷	3−	5−	20+	4÷		8−
35×	24×					63×		
		24×				2−		80×
17+		3÷		14×		20+		
	17+	48×		3−		448×		
		4−		168×				18×
3÷		378×			14+			
3−							3−	
10+			1080×				2−	

82 Moderate +/−/×/÷

210×		3−		3+		8−	2−	3÷
13+		80×			11+			
		9+		3			63×	2−
3+		3÷	17+		2÷			
4−				24×		40×		16×
15+	56×		3÷		14+			
		54×	8	2−	18+		14+	
	2880×						3	
			24×		4−		2÷	

Moderate +/−/×/÷ 83

1−	21×	2÷		3−	3+		2−	17+
		3−			2−			
16+		14+	20+			4÷	2−	
189×			5−	16+			3+	10×
	3−				2÷			
		6+		3÷	2−	1−	27×	4
2÷		17+						
2−	2÷	7−		3÷		1−		4−
		108×			4	2−		

84 Moderate +/−/×/÷

3÷		7	420×			2−	1−	
1440×			3÷				1−	
	2−		1	15×		1−	4÷	3−
13+		4−		9+				
15+	13+	2÷	17+		3+		30×	
				14×	1−	10+	4−	
	19+		7+					8−
6−				17+	378×	21×		
	2÷						1−	

Moderate +/−/×/÷ 85

72×			90×	8−		19+	15+	
2÷	4−			15×			10+	
		648×			2−	3−		8
1−			3−				4÷	
270×	5			3+	1−		18+	
	8−	56×			15+	6×		
		4−				5+		
17+		5+		17+	19+	36×		150×
	3+							

86 Challenging +/−/×/÷

180×		54×	20+			2016×		
		4÷			2−			
12+	168×		4−		2−		8	
3÷				240×			6×	
3−	630×		14+	8−				
10+					8−	4÷	2÷	
336×			15×					
3÷	10+	160×	11+	5−	17+			
		6			120×			

19+		4−		135×		9+		
	2÷		4−		1−		45×	4÷
3−		36×		864×		7		
2−			2−				35×	
14×		1−		4÷		96×		17+
15+		5−	21×		8−			
	135×		7−		11+		2÷	
8−			1−	6+	11+		3÷	
	2−					12+		

88 Challenging +/−/×/÷

2−	32×			3÷	3÷		14+	
	11+	2−			15+	3÷		
6			21+			14×		20+
15+	4−			2÷		8−		
	81×			13+		11+		
		4−			56×		4÷	
	15+	12+			4−	14+		120×
		189×		5−		4−		
64×					3÷		6	

Challenging +/−/×/÷ 89

54×			84×			3−	20×	
224×	12×		13+					16+
	2−		20+	4÷		3÷	5−	
		14+			16+			
			6−				21+	
3÷	4÷	15+						15+
		48×	315×		180×			
4−			48×			12+		
4−				3÷		4	13+	

90 Challenging +/−/×/÷

2−		5−		7−	105×		10+	
3÷	48×	1−			7−		210×	
		9	96×			112×		
10×		1−	3−					8−
24×				12+		3−		
6−	378×			12+	4÷		1−	
	13+	6+				2−	11+	24×
		8+	4÷	360×				
4−					5−		3−	

Challenging +/−/×/÷ 91

40×	2÷		2−	3÷	8+		23+	
	2−				3−	3−		
7	35+	2−		4÷			10+	
24×		17+	5−		17+	3÷		7−
			24×			13+		
1−		2−	5		32×			
		8−	16+		4−		1−	
8−	2÷	4−			4	13+		
			1−		2÷		4÷	

92 Challenging +/−/×/÷

432×			1−		10+	14×	1−
448×	8−	42×					3
		60×			4−	11+	15+
		15+	26+			6	
2−			3÷		252×		48×
20+	2−		14+				3−
			3−	504×			
	7+			2÷	8×		2−
		5−			2÷		2−

Challenging +/−/×/÷ 93

384×		35×			3÷		17+	18+
	13+		24×					
12×		5		15+			11+	
8+		17+		2÷		23+		
	630×	8−		6×	20+			
6−			11+				8−	
				5−		36×	1−	
36×	1−	24+			4−		40×	
		13+				12+		

94 Challenging +/−/×/÷

2−	2−	36×		56×			192×	
			2÷		14+			
64×		3−	11+		6×	15+	2−	42×
	126×			20+				
240×		3÷					10×	
		5−		18+	6×			24×
	11+	630×	15+				5	
3÷					7	192×		14+
				13+				

Challenging +/−/×/÷ 95

4−	8−		4÷		14+	120×		1−
	15+		2÷					
336×			10+	16+		5−	54×	8−
					2÷			
1−	8+	45×	54×			4	4÷	
			6×		420×			5−
4−		6−	6		19+	17+		
6−	10+		16+	14+				9+
						3÷		

96 Challenging +/−/×/÷

18×	64×		22+		13+		
		2−		8+		16+	
8−		1−	12+		16+		1−
810×		48×				40×	
2÷	210×	28×	23+				
					3−	2−	8−
105×	16×	13+	2÷				
		48×		13+	18+		
	16+					4−	

Challenging +/−/×/÷   97

3÷		21+			1176×	72×	8+	
10×								
	2−	8−	36×		1008×			2−
252×				2−		40×	35+	
	23+							14+
		23+						
5	10+			19+		24×		216×
48×		12+		1−				
	3÷							

98 Challenging +/−/×/÷

70×			8−		16+		12×	
4÷		1−	3−		18+		4−	
15+						11+	6	16+
	2÷		19+	560×				
144×	5					11+	4−	15+
		3−		2÷				
63×		2÷			11+	20×	2÷	
5−	6−		3÷				45×	7+
	7−		168×					

3÷		3÷	3402×		4−		2−	
28×	16+			13+		40×		4÷
				6×			3−	
	16+			3−	8−			14+
7−		2÷			7+			
15×	7−	3−		56×	1−		7−	
		2÷			2−	216×		
2−	45×	13+				2÷		6−
		7−		7+		15+		

100 Challenging +/−/×/÷

4−		3−		64×			1	11+
6+		144×		2−		90×		
48×	2÷			15+			210×	
		5−	18+		13+			144×
24×						8−		
5−	12+		48×				17+	6+
	15+	216×	30×					
			35×		15+			
3÷			5−		14×		13+	

ANSWERS

1

¹1	¹⁻4	³⁰ˣ5	2	3
²⁻5	3	³⁺2	1	²⁻4
3	⁶⁺5	³⁻1	¹⁻4	2
²÷2	1	4	3	²⁵ˣ5
4	¹⁻2	3	5	1

2

⁹⁺4	²⁻3	²÷1	¹⁰ˣ2	5
5	1	2	¹²ˣ3	4
⁶⁺1	¹⁵⁺2	4	5	²⁻3
2	⁹⁺5	²⁻3	4	1
3	4	5	¹⁻1	2

3

³3	⁹⁺5	4	⁴ˣ1	2
²÷1	²⁻3	³⁰ˣ5	2	¹⁻4
2	1	3	⁷⁺4	5
¹⁻5	4	2	3	²⁻1
⁸ˣ4	2	1	⁵5	3

4

²⁴ˣ2	4	⁶⁺5	²⁻3	1
3	⁹⁺2	1	²⁰ˣ4	5
³⁻4	5	2	⁴⁻1	¹⁻3
1	¹⁵ˣ3	⁷⁺4	5	2
5	1	3	²÷2	4

5

²÷4	¹¹⁺3	¹⁰ˣ1	5	2
2	4	3	1	⁶⁰ˣ5
⁵ˣ5	1	²÷4	2	3
1	⁷⁺2	5	¹⁻3	4
²⁻3	5	²2	4	1

6

¹⁻4	3	⁶⁰ˣ5	2	6	²÷1
²÷1	²⁻4	6	²⁻3	5	2
2	²⁰ˣ5	4	¹¹⁺1	¹²ˣ3	¹⁻6
⁵⁴⁰ˣ3	³⁺1	2	6	4	5
5	6	¹¹⁺1	4	⁶ˣ2	3
6	2	3	5	⁵⁺1	4

7

6× 6	1	7+ 4	3	3− 5	2
1	40× 2	5	4	2÷ 6	3
24× 2	5 5	1	11+ 6	1− 3	4
4	36× 3	6 6	5	2÷ 2	4− 1
3	6	2	2÷ 1	4	5
12+ 5	4	3	2	6× 1	6

8

6× 2	1	6	5	1− 3	4
3	2÷ 2	1	5− 6	14+ 4	5
1− 4	3	3− 2	1	5	2÷ 6
5− 1	6	5	9+ 4	2	3
15+ 6	60× 5	4	3	4+ 1	2
5	4	3	3÷ 2	6	1

9

20× 5	4	7+ 2	2− 3	1	24× 6
2÷ 2	1	5	3− 6	3	4
1− 3	3+ 2	1	2− 4	1− 6	5
4	1− 6	7+ 3	2	4− 5	1
5− 6	5	4	2÷ 1	2	5+ 3
1	2÷ 3	6	1− 5	4	2

10

3− 1	2÷ 2	4	2− 3	5	36× 6
4	4− 1	5	30× 6	3÷ 2	3
1− 3	10+ 4	1	5	6	2
2	6	3÷ 3	1	1− 4	5
1− 5	10+ 3	3÷ 6	2	1 1	5+ 4
6	5	2	7+ 4	3	1

11

11+ 5	10+ 3	20× 4	5− 6	1	2÷ 2
6	1	5	1− 3	2	4
120× 2	6	1	1− 5	4	3÷ 3
3	5	10+ 2	8× 4	90× 6	1
4	2	6	1	3	5
12× 1	4	3	2	30× 5	6

12

3− 5	2	1− 4	5− 6	1	2÷ 3
24× 4	1	5	5+ 3	2	6
2	5− 6	1	5	6+ 3	60× 4
3	2− 4	2	1	6 6	5
1− 6	5	2÷ 3	2÷ 2	1− 4	2÷ 1
3÷ 1	3	6	4	5	2

13

2− 2	3÷ 3	10× 5	5+ 4	1	1− 6
4	1	2	2− 3	2− 6	5
2÷ 3	5− 6	1	5	4	1− 2
6	2÷ 4	3− 3	9+ 2	12+ 5	1
100× 5	2	6	1	3	4
1	5	4	6	6× 2	3

14

2÷ 2	1	60× 5	3	3− 4	11+ 6
120× 3	2	6 6	4	1	5
4	2− 6	1− 2	5 5	3÷ 3	1
5	4	1	3÷ 2	6	1− 3
5− 6	2− 5	3	10+ 1	2	4
1	72× 3	4	6	5	2

15

4− 5	1	2− 4	2	1− 3	2÷ 6
3− 1	1− 4	5	5− 6	2	3
4	3 3	9+ 6	1	3− 5	2
11+ 6	5	2	12× 3	5+ 1	4
11+ 3	2	1	4	6 6	4− 5
2 2	6	12+ 3	5	4	1

16

1− 3	2	1− 4	5	24× 6	5− 1
12+ 5	1	30× 2	3	4	6
6	4 4	5	1	1− 3	2
2÷ 2	1− 5	6	20× 4	1	1− 3
1	3− 6	3	3÷ 2	5	4
8+ 4	3	1	6	3− 2	5

17

7+ 3	3− 2	5	5− 1	1− 6	48× 4
4	3÷ 1	7+ 3	6	5	2
11+ 5	3	4	2÷ 2	1	6
2	4	3÷ 6	2− 5	3	1 1
30× 1	6	2	1− 3	4	8+ 5
6 6	5	8× 1	4	2	3

18

1− 4	3	1− 5	6	2÷ 2	1
2÷ 2	4	5− 6	1	3 3	15× 5
5− 6	2− 2	4	7+ 5	4− 1	3
1	3− 6	3	2	5	48× 4
2− 3	5	2÷ 1	17+ 4	6	2
6+ 5	1	2	3	4	6

19

6+ 5	72× 4	6	1− 3	2	2÷ 1
1	3	12+ 4	5	7+ 6	2
2− 4	6	3	2 2	1	15+ 5
2− 3	5	60× 2	1	4 4	6
4− 2	2÷ 1	5	6	11+ 3	4
6	2	3− 1	4	5	3

20

540× 6	10+ 4	1	5	1− 3	2
5	6	3	2÷ 4	2	3− 1
24× 3	3− 5	2	5− 6	1	4
2	1	60× 5	13+ 3	4	6
4	2	6	10× 1	5	3 3
12× 1	3	4	2	1− 6	5

21

1− 6	5	6+ 1	3	2	80× 4
12+ 3	60× 6	2	7+ 1	4	5
4	2÷ 2	5	6	54× 3	1
5	1	12+ 3	4	6	2 2
24× 2	4	12+ 6	5	1	3
1	3	4	2	30× 5	6

22

40× 4	2	2÷ 6	3	7+ 1	15× 5
2÷ 6	5	4− 1	2	4	3
3	5− 1	5	13+ 6	3− 2	2− 4
6+ 1	6	3	4	5	2
5	2÷ 4	2	10+ 1	2÷ 3	5− 6
6× 2	3	4	5	6	1

23

18× 3	10+ 1	5	48× 6	4	2
1	6× 2	4	2− 5	3	2− 6
6	3	5+ 2	6+ 1	30× 5	4
1− 4	5	3	2	6	9+ 1
17+ 2	4	6 6	3	2÷ 1	5
5	6	3− 1	4	2	3

24

3÷ 2	6	40× 5	1	4	15× 3
7+ 3	4	2	5− 6	1	5
2− 6	60× 3	4	3− 2	5	1
4	5	3÷ 1	3	3÷ 2	6
6+ 1	2	3	18+ 5	6	2÷ 4
30× 5	1	6	4	3	2

25

3÷ 6	3− 3	5+ 4	1	3− 2	5
2	6	60× 3	4	5	3÷ 1
1− 4	1− 5	4− 1	3÷ 2	6	3
3	4	5	7+ 6	1	48× 2
4− 5	6+ 1	2	3	4	6
1	60× 2	6	5	1− 3	4

26

30× 1	2÷ 4	2	2÷ 3	6	3− 5
5	8+ 3	9+ 4	5− 6	1	2
6	5	3	2	9+ 4	3÷ 1
2− 4	2	5− 6	1	5	3
2÷ 2	1	9+ 5	4	2÷ 3	6
2÷ 3	6	6+ 1	5	2− 2	4

27

2÷ 4	2	1− 6	5	3÷ 3	1
14+ 3	40× 5	4	2	6× 1	6
6	6+ 1	2	3	11+ 4	3− 5
5	1− 4	3	1	6	2
2÷ 1	2÷ 3	20× 5	4− 6	2	4 4
2	6	1	4	2− 5	3

28

75× 5	3	5− 6	1	2÷ 4	2
3− 1	5	2 2	15+ 3	6	1− 4
4	3− 1	3÷ 3	6	30× 2	5
24× 2	4	1	5	3	6 6
6	2	11+ 5	4	6+ 1	2− 3
13+ 3	6	4	2	5	1

29

5− 1	3− 4	200× 5	2	2÷ 3	6
6	1	4	5	7+ 2	3
1− 4	2÷ 6	3	6+ 1	5	2
3	30× 2	9+ 1	10+ 4	6	1− 5
5	3	2	6	1 1	4
3− 2	5	2÷ 6	3	5+ 4	1

30

4− 1	5	6+ 3	2− 4	6	60× 2
1− 4	108× 1	2	10+ 3	5	6
5	6	1	2	7+ 4	3
6	3	10+ 4	5	30× 2	1 1
2÷ 2	4	6	1 1	3	5
1− 3	2	11+ 5	6	5+ 1	4

31

2÷ 6	3	1− 5	11+ 2	4	8× 1
5+ 3	1	6	5	3÷ 2	4
1	2− 5	3	1− 4	6	2
2÷ 4	2	8× 1	3	1− 5	6
13+ 5	4	2	11+ 6	2− 1	3
2	6	4	1	2− 3	5

32

12+ 6	2	15× 5	3	12× 4	1
4	150× 1	6	5	11+ 2	3
2− 3	5	8+ 1	2− 4	6	2
5	4	3	2	1	2− 6
2÷ 1	11+ 3	2	24× 6	15× 5	4
2	6	4	1	3	5 5

33

2− 5	2÷ 4	13+ 3	1− 2	1	5− 6
3	2	6	20× 5	4	1
3÷ 2	6	4	1	8+ 3	10× 5
13+ 6	3	3− 1	4	5	2
4	7+ 1	3− 5	17+ 6	2	1− 3
1	5	2	3	6	4

34

2− 4	6	4− 1	5	1− 2	3
6 6	7+ 2	1− 4	3	12+ 1	5
3	1	60× 5	2	1− 4	6
1	12+ 3	6	4 4	5	2÷ 2
7+ 2	5	1− 3	7+ 1	2÷ 6	4
5	4	2	6	3	1 1

35

60× 2	1 1	10+ 4	1− 5	6	2− 3
5	15× 3	6	2÷ 2	4	1
6	5	24× 2	3	3÷ 1	2− 4
8+ 1	2	5	4	3	6
288× 4	6	10+ 3	6+ 1	5	2 2
3	4	1	6	3− 2	5

36

60× 3	5	4	3÷ 2	6	9+ 1
2÷ 4	2	60× 6	8+ 1	5	3
5− 6	1	2	3	20× 4	5
3÷ 1	3	5	4	1− 2	24× 6
60× 2	6	2− 3	5	1	4
5	11+ 4	1	6	1− 3	2

37

15× 3	7+ 6	36× 2	4− 5	1	4 4
5	1	6	3	12+ 4	2÷ 2
72× 4	3	2− 5	2	6	1
6	2÷ 4	3	2÷ 1	2	13+ 5
1− 1	2	20× 4	2− 6	5	3
2	5	1	4	2÷ 3	6

38

12× 6	1	2 2	12+ 3	4	5
20× 1	2	24× 6	4	11+ 5	3
5	4	1	1− 2	3	3÷ 6
24× 3	1− 5	4	1	4− 6	2
4	2÷ 6	8+ 3	5	2	4× 1
2	3	1− 5	6	1	4

39

11+ 6	2− 5	3− 1	4	24× 2	3
5	3	2÷ 6	1	4	48× 2
8+ 2	1	3	1− 5	6	4
1	2÷ 2	4	3	9+ 5	6
4	30× 6	5	2	3	1
1− 3	4	3÷ 2	6	4− 1	5

40

4− 1	36× 3	6	2− 4	2	2− 5
5	15+ 4	2	1	5− 6	3
2÷ 6	5	11+ 3	3− 2	3− 1	4
3	6	1	5	9+ 4	3÷ 2
7+ 2	1	4	3	5	6
4	13+ 2	5	6	3÷ 3	1

41

40× 4	2	14+ 5	5+ 1	7+ 6	1− 3
5	6	3	4	1	2
3 3	5+ 1	2÷ 4	2	12+ 5	24× 6
1	3	17+ 6	5	2	4
18+ 2	4	1	6	2− 3	5
6	5	2	3	3− 4	1

42

6+ 1	5	10× 2	36× 3	6	1− 4
2− 6	2÷ 4	5	2	1	3
4	2	8+ 3	1	150× 5	6
9+ 2	1	6	4	1− 3	5
2÷ 3	6	30× 1	5	4	4× 2
12+ 5	3	4	6	2	1

43

5 (6+)	1	3 (3)	2 (2÷)	4 (24×)	6
6 (2−)	4 (2÷)	2	1	5 (2−)	3
4	2 (3−)	5	3 (2÷)	6	1 (3−)
3 (11+)	5	1 (11+)	6 (3÷)	2	4
2 (2÷)	3	6	4	1 (1)	5 (3−)
1	6 (2−)	4	5 (2−)	3	2

44

2 (11+)	6	3 (12×)	4	1 (4−)	5
4 (2−)	3	6 (12+)	1	5 (30×)	2
6	1 (2÷)	4 (5+)	5	2 (2)	3
5 (2−)	2	1	3 (11+)	6 (24×)	4
3	5 (20×)	2	6	4 (3−)	1
1	4	5 (3−)	2	3 (3−)	6

45

4 (40×)	6 (5−)	1	5 (11+)	2 (1−)	3
2	5 (1−)	4	6	3 (12×)	1
5	2 (11+)	6	3	1 (6+)	4
3 (18×)	4 (60×)	2 (2÷)	1	5	6 (72×)
1	3	5	4 (2−)	6	2
6	1 (3÷)	3	2	4 (1−)	5

46

5 (90×)	3	2	7 (2−)	1	6 (6−)	4 (2−)
3	2 (5−)	6 (108×)	5	7	4 (3−)	1
4 (2÷)	7	3	6	2 (3+)	1	5 (90×)
2	4 (3−)	7	1 (3−)	5 (5)	3	6
7 (42×)	5 (12+)	1	4	6 (11+)	2	3
1	6	5 (10+)	3 (9+)	4	7 (5−)	2
6	1	4	2	3 (105×)	5	7

47

7 (35×)	2 (84×)	3	1 (10+)	5	4	6 (10+)
5	6 (13+)	2	7	4 (48×)	1	3
1	7	6 (1−)	5	2	3 (1−)	4
4 (10+)	1	7 (6−)	2	3	6 (1−)	5 (12+)
2	3	1	4 (10+)	6	5	7
6 (2−)	4	5 (8+)	3	1 (6−)	7	2 (2÷)
3 (60×)	5	4	6 (1−)	7	2 (2)	1

48

5 (30×)	2	4 (13+)	1	7 (6−)	3	6 (2÷)
3	1	5	4 (72×)	6	2	7 (2−)
2 (24×)	7 (42×)	1	3 (1−)	4	6	5
4	3	6	5 (5)	2 (2÷)	7 (21×)	1
6 (1−)	5	2 (14×)	7	1 (13+)	4 (60×)	3
1 (6−)	4 (2−)	7	6	3	5	2 (12+)
7	6	3 (1−)	2	5	1	4

49

10× 2	5	1	16+ 6	11+ 7	4	3÷ 3
2− 7	12+ 2	3	4	6	90× 5	1
5	7	3+ 2	1	1− 4	3	6
3÷ 1	3	13+ 4	2	5	6 6	56× 7
2÷ 3	1	6	7+ 5	2	6− 7	4
6	4 4	22+ 5	4− 7	3÷ 3	1	2
4	6	7	3	1	3− 2	5

50

2− 5	3− 7	2	24× 6	4	3÷ 1	3
3	4	5	3+ 2	1	3÷ 6	1− 7
1− 4	3	1 1	16+ 7	5	2	6
3÷ 6	1− 2	3	4	13+ 7	4− 5	1
2	30× 1	11+ 7	3	6	9+ 4	5
8+ 7	5	6	1	1− 2	3	2− 4
1	10+ 6	4	15× 5	3	7 7	2

51

126× 7	3− 4	1	15× 3	5	3÷ 2	6
3	6	12+ 4	2	84× 7	6+ 1	5
6− 1	7	8+ 5	6	3	4	2÷ 2
10× 5	2	3	28× 4	1− 6	7	1
2÷ 2	11+ 5	13+ 6	7	1	3− 3	1− 4
4	1	7	3− 5	2	6	3
6 6	3	2	3− 1	4	2− 5	7

52

1− 4	17+ 7	6	2÷ 1	2	15× 5	3
5	4	1− 1	5− 2	11+ 7	2÷ 3	6
3÷ 3	10× 5	2	7	4	30× 6	1
1	2	72× 3	4	1− 6	7	5
1− 2	1	5 5	6	2− 3	3− 4	7
1− 7	6	28× 4	9+ 3	5	2÷ 1	2
2÷ 6	3	7	5	1	2÷ 2	4

53

210× 6	7	1− 2	3	1− 4	3− 1	35× 5
5	3÷ 2	6	13+ 7	3	4	1
2− 4	8+ 3	5 5	6	3+ 1	2	7
2	4	1	3− 5	15+ 7	2÷ 6	3
2− 1	420× 5	3	2	6	3− 7	4
3	6× 1	7	10+ 4	2	15× 5	3÷ 6
7 7	6	4	1	5	3	2

54

60× 4	2− 5	13+ 6	7	3÷ 1	3	1− 2
5	7	7+ 1	3÷ 2	2÷ 4	1− 6	3
3	1	5	6	2	7	16× 4
13+ 7	2− 2	14+ 3	5	6	4	1
6	4	8+ 7	1	5+ 3	2	1− 5
3÷ 1	3	2− 2	3− 4	7	13+ 5	6
3÷ 2	6	4	2− 3	5	1	7

55

2− **3**	**5**	28× **4**	**7**	3÷ **2**	**6**	11+ **1**
5− **2**	**7**	3÷ **1**	**3**	90× **6**	**5**	**4**
3− **1**	**4**	9+ **2**	35× **5**	**7**	**3**	**6**
13+ **7**	**1**	**3**	1− **6**	**5**	2− **4**	**2**
6	**3**	8+ **7**	**1**	3− **4**	3− **2**	**5**
10× **5**	**2**	2− **6**	**4**	**1**	10+ **7**	**3**
2− **4**	**6**	10+ **5**	**2**	**3**	6− **1**	**7**

56

40× **5**	**8**	2÷ **2**	**1**	**6**	3− **3**	2− **7**	20+ **4**
2÷ **3**	**6**	2÷ **4**	**2**	7− **1**	**8**	**5**	**7**
6× **2**	**3**	28× **7**	**4**	40× **5**	6 **6**	**8**	**1**
2÷ **4**	**2**	**1**	3− **5**	**8**	42× **7**	**6**	54× **3**
5− **1**	2− **7**	2− **5**	**8**	13+ **2**	**4**	**3**	**6**
6	**5**	**3**	336× **7**	**4**	3+ **1**	4÷ **2**	**8**
3− **7**	**4**	**8**	**6**	**3**	**2**	6+ **1**	**5**
7− **8**	**1**	3− **6**	**3**	280× **7**	**5**	**4**	**2**

57

4− **7**	2− **4**	**6**	80× **2**	**8**	9+ **3**	**1**	**5**
3	20+ **8**	**1**	**5**	140× **4**	**7**	84× **2**	**6**
8	**3**	240× **4**	3+ **1**	**2**	**5**	16+ **6**	**7**
2	**6**	**5**	15+ **8**	**7**	3− **4**	**3**	3÷ **1**
21+ **4**	**2**	**8**	1− **6**	**5**	**1**	**7**	**3**
30× **1**	**7**	3 **3**	504× **4**	**6**	3− **2**	**5**	4÷ **8**
6	4− **5**	**7**	**3**	7− **1**	**8**	768× **4**	**2**
5	**1**	5− **2**	**7**	3 **3**	**6**	**8**	**4**

58

3+ **2**	**1**	2− **8**	48× **3**	42× **7**	**6**	3− **4**	1680× **5**
2− **5**	11+ **3**	**6**	**8**	**2**	1− **4**	**1**	**7**
3	**2**	2÷ **4**	8+ **7**	**1**	**5**	**6**	**8**
15+ **8**	**6**	**2**	1− **5**	21× **3**	**1**	**7**	2÷ **4**
7	4÷ **4**	**1**	**6**	24× **8**	**3**	3− **5**	**2**
4÷ **4**	2− **5**	**7**	6× **1**	**6**	6− **2**	**8**	3− **3**
1	1680× **7**	60× **3**	**4**	**5**	**8**	2 **2**	**6**
6	**8**	**5**	13+ **2**	**4**	**7**	3÷ **3**	**1**

59

4÷ **2**	1− **3**	30× **6**	**5**	3÷ **1**	26+ **4**	**8**	**7**
8	**4**	3+ **1**	**2**	**3**	2− **5**	**7**	15+ **6**
24+ **6**	**8**	7 **7**	2÷ **1**	**2**	**3**	12+ **5**	**4**
7 **7**	**2**	**8**	48× **3**	**4**	**6**	**1**	**5**
3÷ **1**	30× **6**	**5**	**4**	42× **7**	**2**	**3**	8 **8**
3	**1**	3− **4**	**7**	3− **5**	**8**	4− **6**	1− **2**
9+ **4**	**5**	13+ **3**	336× **6**	**8**	**7**	**2**	**1**
2− **5**	**7**	**2**	**8**	5− **6**	**1**	1− **4**	**3**

60

60× **4**	14× **2**	**7**	40× **1**	**5**	**8**	2÷ **3**	**6**
5	**3**	**1**	13+ **2**	**6**	1− **7**	1− **4**	15+ **8**
3÷ **6**	3− **4**	**3**	**8**	3+ **2**	**1**	**5**	**7**
2	**7**	9+ **5**	**4**	2÷ **3**	**6**	7− **8**	**1**
120× **3**	**8**	2− **6**	2− **5**	**7**	2÷ **2**	**1**	2÷ **4**
15+ **8**	**5**	**4**	17+ **7**	3÷ **1**	**3**	6 **6**	**2**
7	16× **1**	**8**	**6**	**4**	3− **5**	**2**	2− **3**
5− **1**	**6**	**2**	5− **3**	**8**	3− **4**	**7**	**5**

61

21×7	3÷2	6	400×8	4+3	1	4	1−5
3	14+6	4	2	5	7−8	1	42×7
7−8	4	1−2	5	1·1	1−3	140×7	6
1	15+7	3	14+6	8	4	5	2
12+4	8	8+1	7	1−6	3−5	2	2−3
5	3	15+8	4	7	2	2−6	1
13+6	13+1	5	3	9+2	7	8	2÷4
2	5	7	3−1	4	2÷6	3	8

62

2·2	15+7	8	1−1	3÷3	1−5	6	64×4
3−7	2−5	3	2	1	24×6	4	8
4	2÷3	6	3−8	5	1	210×7	2
12×1	4÷8	2	4−3	3−7	4	5	6
3	4	140×1	7	3÷6	2	3−8	5
480×6	2	7	11+5	4	15+8	1	7+3
8	5−6	5	4	2	7	3	6−1
5	1	2−4	6	8·8	5+3	2	7

63

96×6	2	4·4	60×3	5	8	1−1	7
8	3−5	5+3	2	4	7	6	3÷1
10×5	8	17+6	4	7	3+1	2	3
2	13+6	7	7−1	8	40×5	14+3	2÷4
3÷3	3+1	2	1−5	6	4	7	8
1	11+7	7−8	6	13+3	2	4	13+5
3−7	4	1	8	2	2÷3	3−5	6
4	2−3	5	7	1	6	8	2

64

126×7	6	3+1	2	4	5	12×3	2−8
1	3	1680×7	5	8	8+2	4	6
1−5	15+7	8	6	2	4	9+1	3
6	64×8	4	84×7	3	2÷1	2	5
11+3	2	15+6	4	2−5	15+8	7	3+1
8	4	5	7−1	7	16+3	6	2
2÷2	3÷1	3	8	13+6	7	1−5	4
4	3−5	2	3·3	1	6	1−8	7

65

84×7	3	2÷4	2	7−1	8	1680×6	5
4	12+5	6×2	16+3	6	1	8	7
6	1	3	7	140×4	5	7+2	96×8
3÷3	2−6	8	3+1	2	7	5	4
1	3÷2	6	18+8	5	48×4	7·7	3
392×8	7	1	5	17+3	6	72×4	2÷2
1−5	4	7	6	8	2	3	1
4÷2	8	20×5	4	4−7	3	1	6

66

24×1	2−4	2	24+5	7	6+3	1−6	5−8
4	6	1−7	8	1	2	5	3
4÷2	8	6	4	140×5	7	5−3	10+1
16+7	5·5	4÷1	54×6	3	4	8	2
8	1	4	3	17+6	5	2÷2	7
2÷3	48×2	8	7	3−4	6	1	120×5
6	3	3−5	2	4÷8	7−1	7	3−4
2−5	7	3÷3	1	2	8	4	6

67

288× 3	6	16+ 8	5− 2	7	1− 5	4	20× 1
2	8	1	7	4÷ 4	4− 6	2− 3	5
21+ 8	4− 3	1− 7	6	1	2	5	4
6	7	1− 4	2− 3	5	7− 8	1	36× 2
7	8× 1	5	18+ 8	6	4	4÷ 2	3
1 1	4	2÷ 3	1− 5	1− 2	6− 7	8	6
20× 5	2	6	4	3	1	22+ 7	8
4	3− 5	2	9+ 1	8	2÷ 3	6	7

68

5− 2	7	5− 3	8	6+ 1	5	10+ 4	384× 6
2− 5	3	14+ 7	6	4÷ 8	2	1	4
32× 8	4	6	18+ 1	35× 5	7	3	2
1	3− 5	4	3	56× 7	7+ 6	2	8
6 6	8	5	4	2	1	18+ 7	15× 3
24× 4	6	20+ 2	7	3	8	5	1
21× 7	1	13+ 8	2	15+ 4	1− 3	6	5
3	2	1	5	6	4	56× 8	7

69

35× 5	1− 2	15× 3	17+ 4	7	6	7− 8	1
7	3	5	96× 6	2	8	1	2− 4
48× 8	1	196× 4	7	30× 3	2	5	6
3	26+ 5	7	40× 1	2÷ 8	19+ 4	6	2
2	6	8	5	4	11+ 1	3	7
4÷ 1	7	4÷ 2	8	7+ 6	3	4	120× 5
4	8	12× 6	2	1	2− 5	9+ 7	3
10+ 6	4	1	2− 3	5	7	2	8

70

30× 6	5	84× 7	4	3	8	7− 1	2÷ 2
5− 8	3	6− 1	7	3− 2	5	2− 6	4
4÷ 1	14+ 2	2− 5	336× 6	8	7	4	21× 3
4	8	3	18+ 5	6	2÷ 1	2	7
4− 7	4	19+ 8	2	5	17+ 6	2− 3	1 1
3	7	4	8	1	2	5	48× 6
3− 5	7+ 6	10+ 2	1	4	3	20+ 7	8
2	1	2÷ 6	3	3− 7	4	8	5

71

3÷ 6	320× 8	10+ 1	4	2	3	4− 5	3− 7
2	5	8	36× 6	84× 3	13+ 7	1	4
2÷ 8	3	2	1	4	5	5− 7	1− 6
4	84× 6	5− 3	8	7	1	2	5
7	2	60× 6	5	1	12+ 4	11+ 8	3÷ 3
105× 5	7	9+ 4	2	8 8	6	3	1
3	15+ 1	5	18+ 7	6	2	192× 4	6− 8
1 1	4	7	3	5	8	6	2

72

35× 7	26+ 5	1− 3	2	3÷ 1	6	18+ 4	2÷ 8
5	6	6− 1	7	3	4	8	5− 2
3÷ 2	8	30× 5	6	7+ 4	3	10+ 1	7
6	7	16+ 4	7− 8	4− 2	5	3	1
16+ 3	4	8	1	6	8+ 2	12+ 7	5
4	2÷ 2	21× 7	3	13+ 8	1	5	2÷ 6
8	1	15+ 6	4	5	784× 7	2	3
1	1− 3	2	5	7	8	2− 6	4

73

7	6	1	5	3	4	8	2
3	1	2	8	4	7	6	5
6	8	3	4	2	5	7	1
1	5	4	6	8	2	3	7
2	7	6	3	1	8	5	4
4	2	5	7	6	3	1	8
5	4	8	1	7	6	2	3
8	3	7	2	5	1	4	6

74

8	5	4	3	2	7	6	1
7	1	2	8	3	6	5	4
5	8	1	6	7	3	4	2
3	7	5	1	4	2	8	6
1	4	6	7	5	8	2	3
2	6	3	5	8	4	1	7
6	2	7	4	1	5	3	8
4	3	8	2	6	1	7	5

75

5	8	4	6	3	2	7	1
4	6	3	5	1	7	8	2
3	2	1	8	5	6	4	7
1	4	5	7	6	8	2	3
7	1	6	3	2	4	5	8
8	3	2	4	7	1	6	5
2	7	8	1	4	5	3	6
6	5	7	2	8	3	1	4

76

3	2	1	5	9	4	8	7	6
4	5	3	6	8	1	2	9	7
5	3	7	1	6	8	4	2	9
8	1	4	7	5	9	3	6	2
1	4	2	9	7	3	6	8	5
6	7	9	4	1	2	5	3	8
9	6	5	8	2	7	1	4	3
2	9	8	3	4	6	7	5	1
7	8	6	2	3	5	9	1	4

77

8	3	6	5	7	1	9	4	2
3	7	2	1	4	5	6	8	9
7	9	3	2	1	8	4	6	5
2	4	8	6	5	7	3	9	1
1	5	7	8	6	9	2	3	4
6	8	4	7	9	2	5	1	3
9	2	1	3	8	4	7	5	6
5	1	9	4	3	6	8	2	7
4	6	5	9	2	3	1	7	8

78

7	4	9	6	3	2	8	1	5
4	6	7	9	5	1	3	8	2
6	1	8	5	4	7	9	2	3
8	3	1	2	6	5	7	9	4
9	7	3	4	1	6	2	5	8
1	2	5	8	7	9	4	3	6
2	5	6	3	8	4	1	7	9
3	9	4	7	2	8	5	6	1
5	8	2	1	9	3	6	4	7

79

8 ²⁴ˣ	3 ²⁹⁴ˣ	7	2	9 ⁹	1 ²⁴ˣ	6	5	4 ¹⁻
3	7	2 ³⁻	5	8 ²÷	4	1 ⁷⁺	6	9 ⁶³ˣ
5 ³⁰ˣ	6	1 ³÷	3	4	2 ⁴⁸ˣ	8 ²¹⁺	9	7
2 ²÷	9 ⁸⁶⁴ˣ	5 ¹⁴⁺	6 ⁴²ˣ	7	8	3	4	1
4	2	9	8 ¹⁷⁺	3 ³÷	7 ²⁻	5	1 ⁵⁻	6
6	8	3 ³	9	1	5 ¹⁻	4	7 ⁴²ˣ	2 ⁴÷
7 ¹⁷⁺	5	4	1 ⁴÷	6 ³⁻	9	2	3	8
9 ⁸⁻	1	8	4	5 ¹⁻	6	7 ⁶³ˣ	2	3
1	4	6 ¹⁻	7	2 ¹⁻	3	9	8 ³⁻	5

80

1 ⁴⁻	5	3 ³÷	6	8 ⁴⁸ˣ	4	7 ⁵⁶ˣ	2 ¹⁸ˣ	9
5 ¹¹⁺	6	1	7 ²⁸ˣ	4	3	2 ⁴⁻	9 ¹⁷⁺	8 ⁷⁻
3 ²⁴ˣ	4	5 ¹⁰ˣ	2	6 ¹⁹⁺	7	9 ¹⁷⁺	8	1
2	9 ¹⁵⁺	4	1 ¹²⁺	7	6	8	3 ²÷	5 ¹⁻
8 ²¹⁺	7	2	3	1 ⁴⁻	9 ⁸⁻	5 ⁵	6	4
6	2 ¹⁴⁺	9	8	5	1	3 ²⁻	4	7 ¹³⁺
4 ²⁵²ˣ	3	6 ¹²⁰ˣ	5	9 ⁷²ˣ	8	1	7 ³⁵ˣ	2
9	8 ¹⁻	7	4	2 ²	5 ¹²⁰ˣ	6	1	3 ²÷
7	1	8 ¹⁻	9	3 ⁶ˣ	2	4	5	6

81

4 ²⁸ˣ	7	1 ⁴÷	5 ³⁻	3	6 ⁵⁻	2 ²⁰⁺	8 ⁴÷	9 ⁸⁻
5 ³⁵ˣ	6 ²⁴ˣ	4	2	8	3	9 ⁶³ˣ	7	1
7	1	6 ²⁴ˣ	4	9	2	5 ²⁻	3	8 ⁸⁰ˣ
8 ¹⁷⁺	4	3 ³÷	1	2 ¹⁴ˣ	7	6 ²⁰⁺	9	5
9	3 ¹⁷⁺	8 ⁴⁸ˣ	6	1	4 ³⁻	7	5	2 ⁴⁴⁸ˣ
6	8	5 ⁴⁻	9	7 ¹⁶⁸ˣ	1	4	2	3 ¹⁸ˣ
3 ³÷	9	2 ³⁷⁸ˣ	7	4	5 ¹⁴⁺	8	1	6
2 ³⁻	5	9	3	6	8	1	4 ³⁻	7
1 ¹⁰⁺	2	7	8 ¹⁰⁸⁰ˣ	5	9	3	6 ²⁻	4

82

6 ²¹⁰ˣ	5	4 ³⁻	7	2	1 ³⁺	9 ⁸⁻	8 ²⁻	3 ³÷
3 ¹³⁺	7	2 ⁸⁰ˣ	5	8	4 ¹¹⁺	1	6	9
4	6	8 ⁹⁺	1	3 ³	2	5	9 ⁶³ˣ	7 ²⁻
2 ³⁺	1	3 ³÷	6 ¹⁷⁺	9	8 ²÷	4	7	5
7 ⁴⁻	3	9	2	4 ²⁴ˣ	6	8 ⁴⁰ˣ	5	1 ¹⁶ˣ
9 ¹⁵⁺	4 ⁵⁶ˣ	7	3 ³÷	1	5 ¹⁴⁺	6	2	8
5	2	1 ⁵⁴ˣ	8 ⁸	7 ²⁻	9	3 ¹⁸⁺	4	6
1	8 ²⁸⁸⁰ˣ	6	9	5	7	2	3 ³	4
8	9	5 ²⁴ˣ	4	6	3 ⁴⁻	7	1 ²÷	2

83

5 ¹⁻	7 ²¹ˣ	6 ²÷	3	4 ³⁻	2 ³⁺	1	8 ²⁻	9 ¹⁷⁺
4	3	5 ³⁻	2	1	7 ²⁻	9	6	8
1 ¹⁶⁺	9	3 ¹⁴⁺	7 ²⁰⁺	5	8	2 ⁴÷	4	6
3 ¹⁸⁹ˣ	6	4	9 ⁵⁻	7	1	8	2 ³⁺	5 ¹⁰ˣ
9	5 ³⁻	7	4	8	6 ²÷	3	1	2
7	8	1 ⁶⁺	5	2 ³÷	3	6 ¹⁻	9 ²⁷ˣ	4 ⁴
2 ²÷	4	9 ¹⁷⁺	8	6	5	7	3	1
6 ²⁻	2 ²÷	8 ⁷⁻	1	3 ³÷	9	4 ¹⁻	5	7 ⁴⁻
8	1	2 ¹⁰⁸ˣ	6	9	4 ⁴	5	7	3

84

1 ³÷	3	7	6 ⁴²⁰ˣ	5	2	4 ²⁻	9	8 ¹⁻
4 ¹⁴⁴⁰ˣ	8	5	7	9 ³÷	3	6	1 ¹⁻	2
9	2 ²⁻	4	1 ¹	3 ¹⁵ˣ	5	7 ¹⁻	8 ⁴÷	6 ³⁻
6 ¹³⁺	7	9 ⁴⁻	5	1 ⁹⁺	4	8	2	3
7 ¹⁵⁺	9 ¹³⁺	3 ²÷	8 ¹⁷⁺	4	1 ³⁺	2	6 ³⁰ˣ	5
5	4	6	9	2 ¹⁴ˣ	8 ¹⁻	1 ¹⁰⁺	3	7 ⁴⁻
3	6 ¹⁹⁺	8	2 ⁷⁺	7	9	5	4	1 ⁸⁻
2 ⁶⁻	5	1	4	8 ¹⁷⁺	6 ³⁷⁸ˣ	3 ²¹ˣ	7	9
8	1 ²÷	2	3	6	7	9 ¹⁻	5	4

85

⁷²ˣ3	4	6	⁹⁰ˣ2	⁸⁻9	1	¹⁹⁺5	8	¹⁵⁺7
²÷4	⁴⁻7	5	9	¹⁵ˣ3	6	8	¹⁰⁺1	2
2	3	⁶⁴⁸ˣ9	1	5	²⁻4	³⁻6	7	⁸8
¹⁻7	6	3	³⁻5	8	2	9	⁴÷4	1
²⁷⁰ˣ9	⁵5	4	6	1	³⁺8	¹⁻7	¹⁸⁺2	3
5	⁸⁻9	⁵⁶ˣ7	8	2	¹⁵⁺3	⁶ˣ1	6	4
6	1	⁴⁻8	4	7	5	⁵⁺2	3	9
¹⁷⁺1	8	⁵⁺2	3	¹⁷⁺6	7	³⁶ˣ4	¹⁹⁺9	¹⁵⁰ˣ5
8	³⁺2	1	7	4	9	3	5	6

86

¹⁸⁰ˣ4	5	⁵⁴ˣ9	²⁰⁺1	2	3	²⁰¹⁶ˣ6	8	7
9	3	2	⁴÷4	1	8	²⁻5	7	6
¹²⁺2	4	¹⁶⁸ˣ1	3	5	⁴⁻6	7	9	⁸8
6	³÷2	8	7	9	²⁴⁰ˣ4	3	5	⁶ˣ1
³⁻5	6	⁶³⁰ˣ7	9	8	¹⁴⁺1	⁸⁻4	2	3
8	¹⁰⁺7	3	5	6	9	⁸⁻1	⁴÷4	²÷2
³³⁶ˣ7	8	6	2	¹⁵ˣ3	5	9	1	4
³÷3	¹⁰⁺1	¹⁶⁰ˣ5	8	¹¹⁺4	⁵⁻7	¹⁷⁺2	6	9
1	9	4	⁶6	7	2	¹²⁰ˣ8	3	5

87

¹⁹⁺8	4	⁴⁻3	7	¹³⁵ˣ9	5	⁹⁺6	1	2
7	²÷2	1	⁴⁻6	3	¹⁻8	9	⁴⁵ˣ5	⁴÷4
³⁻5	8	³⁶ˣ4	2	⁸⁶⁴ˣ6	3	⁷7	9	1
²⁻3	1	9	²⁻4	2	6	8	³⁵ˣ7	5
¹⁴ˣ2	7	¹⁻6	5	⁴÷4	1	⁹⁶ˣ3	8	¹⁷⁺9
¹⁵⁺6	5	⁵⁻2	²¹ˣ3	7	⁸⁻9	1	4	8
4	¹³⁵ˣ9	7	⁷⁻1	8	2	5	²÷6	3
⁸⁻9	3	5	¹⁻8	1	⁶⁺7	¹¹⁺4	2	³÷6
1	²⁻6	8	9	5	4	¹²⁺2	3	7

88

²⁻9	³²ˣ4	8	1	³÷3	6	³÷2	5	¹⁴⁺7
7	¹¹⁺5	6	4	1	¹⁵⁺8	³÷9	3	2
⁶6	1	5	²¹⁺8	4	3	¹⁴ˣ7	2	²⁰⁺9
¹⁵⁺5	6	2	7	²÷8	4	1	⁸⁻9	3
1	⁸¹ˣ9	3	6	5	¹³⁺2	4	¹¹⁺7	8
2	3	⁴⁻9	5	6	⁵⁶ˣ7	8	⁴÷4	1
3	¹⁵⁺7	¹²⁺1	2	9	⁴⁻5	6	¹⁴⁺8	¹²⁰ˣ4
4	8	¹⁸⁹ˣ7	3	2	⁵⁻9	5	1	6
⁶⁴ˣ8	2	4	9	7	³÷1	3	⁶6	5

89

⁵⁴ˣ6	1	9	⁸⁴ˣ7	4	3	³⁻8	5	²⁰ˣ2
²²⁴ˣ8	¹²ˣ4	3	1	¹³⁺6	7	5	2	¹⁶⁺9
7	²⁻5	1	²⁰⁺9	⁴÷2	8	³÷6	3	⁵⁻4
1	7	¹⁴⁺4	6	5	¹⁶⁺9	2	8	3
4	3	7	⁶⁻2	8	6	1	²¹⁺9	5
³÷9	⁴÷8	¹⁵⁺5	4	1	2	3	¹⁵⁺7	6
3	2	⁴⁸ˣ6	³¹⁵ˣ5	7	¹⁸⁰ˣ4	9	1	8
²2	6	8	⁴⁸ˣ3	9	5	¹²⁺7	4	1
⁴⁻5	9	2	8	³÷3	1	⁴4	¹³⁺6	7

90

²⁻6	4	⁵⁻8	3	⁷⁻9	¹⁰⁵ˣ7	5	¹⁰⁺1	2
³÷9	⁴⁸ˣ8	¹⁻4	5	2	1	⁷⁻3	²¹⁰ˣ6	7
3	6	⁹9	⁹⁶ˣ4	1	8	¹¹²ˣ2	7	5
¹⁰ˣ2	5	¹⁻3	9	³⁻4	6	7	8	⁸⁻1
²⁴ˣ8	3	2	6	¹²⁺7	5	1	³⁻4	9
⁶⁻1	³⁷⁸ˣ9	6	7	¹²⁺3	⁴÷2	8	5	¹⁻4
7	¹³⁺2	⁶⁺5	1	6	3	²⁻4	9	¹¹⁺8
4	7	⁸⁺1	⁴÷8	³⁶⁰ˣ5	9	6	2	²⁴ˣ3
⁴⁻5	1	7	2	8	⁵⁻4	9	³⁻3	6

91

40×	2÷		2−	3÷	8+			23+
5	4	2	8	6	7	1	9	3
8	3	1	6	2	5	9	7	4
7	8	5	3	4	2	6	1	9
4	5	9	7	1	3	2	6	8
6	7	8	2	3	9	5	4	1
3	9	6	5	8	1	4	2	7
2	6	4	1	9	8	7	3	5
1	2	3	9	7	4	8	5	6
9	1	7	4	5	6	3	8	2

92

6	8	9	5	4	1	2	7	3
8	9	7	6	1	4	5	3	2
4	1	6	2	5	7	3	8	9
2	7	4	8	9	3	6	1	5
5	3	1	9	2	6	7	4	8
7	4	3	1	8	5	9	2	6
3	6	2	4	7	9	8	5	1
9	2	5	7	3	8	1	6	4
1	5	8	3	6	2	4	9	7

93

6	8	1	7	5	9	3	4	2
8	9	4	3	1	6	5	2	7
3	4	5	8	6	7	2	1	9
5	1	8	9	4	2	6	7	3
2	5	9	1	3	8	7	6	4
7	6	3	5	2	4	8	9	1
1	7	2	4	8	3	9	5	6
9	3	6	2	7	1	4	8	5
4	2	7	6	9	5	1	3	8

94

9	5	3	2	1	8	7	6	4
7	3	6	4	2	5	9	8	1
2	8	5	6	4	3	1	9	7
4	9	8	1	3	2	5	7	6
6	7	1	3	8	9	4	2	5
5	2	4	9	7	6	3	1	8
8	4	9	7	6	1	2	5	3
3	1	2	8	5	7	6	4	9
1	6	7	5	9	4	8	3	2

95

5	9	1	8	2	3	6	4	7
1	3	7	4	8	9	2	5	6
7	2	3	1	4	5	8	6	9
6	8	4	5	7	2	3	9	1
3	7	5	9	6	1	4	8	2
4	1	9	2	3	6	5	7	8
9	5	8	6	1	4	7	2	3
8	6	2	3	5	7	9	1	4
2	4	6	7	9	8	1	3	5

96

9	8	2	7	1	5	3	6	4
2	4	3	5	9	7	1	8	6
1	9	4	3	5	6	7	2	8
6	3	5	8	2	1	9	4	7
4	7	9	1	3	8	6	5	2
8	5	6	4	7	9	2	3	1
3	2	7	6	8	4	5	1	9
7	1	8	2	6	3	4	9	5
5	6	1	9	4	2	8	7	3

97

3÷ 3	9	21+ 5	6	2	1176× 7	72× 8	4	8+ 1
10× 2	5	8	7	4	6	9	1	3
1	2÷ 4	8− 9	36× 3	6	1008× 8	7	2	2÷ 5
252× 4	6	1	2	2÷ 3	9	40× 5	35+ 8	7
9	23+ 3	7	1	5	4	2	6	14+ 8
7	8	4	23+ 9	1	2	3	5	6
5	10+ 1	2	8	19+ 9	3	24× 6	7	216× 4
48× 6	7	12+ 3	5	8	1	4	9	2
8	3÷ 2	6	4	7	5	1	3	9

98

70× 2	7	5	8− 1	9	8	6	16+ 3	12× 4
4÷ 1	4	6	3− 8	5	9	2	18+ 7	4− 3
15+ 5	1	7	3	2	4	11+ 8	6 6	16+ 9
9	2÷ 2	4	19+ 7	560× 8	5	3	1	6
144× 6	5 5	3	9	7	2	11+ 1	4− 4	15+ 8
4	6	3− 2	5	2÷ 3	1	9	8	7
63× 7	9	8	4	6	11+ 3	20× 5	2÷ 2	1
5− 8	6− 3	9	3÷ 6	1	7	4	45× 5	7+ 2
3	7− 8	1	2	168× 4	6	7	9	5

99

3÷ 2	6	3÷ 1	3402× 7	9	8	4	2− 3	5
28× 1	16+ 4	3	9	13+ 6	7	40× 8	5	4÷ 2
4	7	5	6× 6	1	2	3	3− 9	8
7	16+ 3	8	5	2	9	1	6	14+ 4
9	2	2÷ 4	8	5	7+ 1	6	7	3
15× 3	7− 1	3− 7	4	56× 8	1− 6	5	7− 2	9
5	8	2÷ 2	1	7	2− 3	216× 9	4	6
2− 8	45× 9	13+ 6	3	4	5	2÷ 2	1	6− 7
6	5	7− 9	2	7+ 3	4	15+ 7	8	1

100

4− 5	9	3− 3	6	64× 4	8	2	1 1	11+ 7
6+ 1	5	144× 8	2	7	9	90× 6	3	4
48× 8	2÷ 2	1	9	15+ 3	4	5	210× 7	6
6	1	2	5− 4	18+ 8	7	13+ 3	5	144× 9
24× 4	6	7	5	9	3	8− 1	2	8
5− 2	12+ 7	5	48× 8	1	6	9	17+ 4	6+ 3
7	8	15+ 6	216× 3	30× 2	5	4	9	1
3	4	9	35× 7	5	15+ 1	8	6	2
3÷ 9	3	4	5− 1	6	14× 2	7	13+ 8	5